Moonlight And You

~ David Jones ~

David Jones was born in 1989 in Liverpool, which is still his home. He studied English Language and Literature at the University of Liverpool, before specialising in Renaissance and Eighteenth Century Literature. He started writing at an early age, and has published four poetry books (Could You Ever Live Without?, Love And Space Dust, Love As The Stars Went Out and Highway Heart) and a novella called Death's Door. He is also a filmmaker, playwright and actor, and is currently completing work on a full length novel.

For more information on the writer, visit: www.storydj.com, twitter @djthedavid or on Facebook at https:// www.facebook.com/davidjoneswriter and @storydj Instagram. He also uploads weekly videos at http:// www.youtube.com/storydj.

ISBN-13: 978-1546406259

ISBN-10: 1546406255

I am sick
To my soul

With a disease
Called
Thought.

She was

The prettiest

"What if?"

She was

A reason

To start

Again.

There was
Forever
In those
Eyes.

The art
Of life
Is letting
Go.

Worlds change
Where eyes
Meet.

How easy
It was
To fall
For you.

You were

Never mine

To lose,

But I

Lost you

all the same.

We search

For the feelings

That will

Destroy us

In the end.

I never
Wanted to
Look back
And say:

"What if?"

I knew I was
In love.

I was thinking
About you
Without even
Trying to.

At last.

I no longer
Needed
The past.

Forever

Can be the

Happiest,

Or the

Saddest

Word.

Love changed
Everything.
It even changed
Me.

"It doesn't get easier." A Four Word Short Story.

How can I
Love someone new,
When every night
I dream
Of you?

There was
Fire in her
Soul and
Love in
Her eyes.

I was
Searching in
Your eyes
For something
That was never
There.

Some times
Things end
Long before
They begin.

We can

Die a thousand times

In one

Lifetime.

I smiled.

We were
Under the
Same sky
At least.

I fell
For you
And I am
Still
Falling.

Was I
Too soft,
Or was
The world
Too hard?

The things
We love
The most,
Hurt us
The most.

Yesterday it
Felt like
The end of
The world,

Today it felt
Like the
Beginning.

You gave
Me poison, and
I drank it so
Willingly.

She was
Her own star,
Shining bright
In the dark.

"I never used to feel like this" A Seven Word Short Story.

Love and
Heartbreak
Are two
Sides of
The same
Coin.

I smiled.
It was time
To move
On.

I don't want
A fairytale
I just want
You.

We'll never
Have forever,
So we
Might as well
Live now.

How can I
Love someone new,
When every night
I dream
Of you?

The stars
Are proof that
Even on the
Darkest night
There is
A little light.

She was not
The answer,
But she made
Me forget all
My questions.

It is
Enough
That she
Exists.

"Falling leaves remind me of you."

Sometimes home
Can be
Another person.

Love is

The cure

And the

Disease.

I was missing you
Before we
Even met.

She was
The dream
I never
Wanted to
Wake up
From.

How easy
It was
To fall
In love
With you.

What is
Forever?
A moment
With
You.

The world

Is different

After a storm:

Perhaps even

Better.

In your eyes

Did I see

The beginning

Or the end?

The stars
Were jealous.
She stole
All their
Light.

I wish
I had lied
When
I said:

"I love you."

It did not
Make sense,
But love
Never does.

I was running
Out of
Miracles, but
Then I met
You.

You were
Never my dream
To dream.

The sky

Was vast

But my heart

Was

Broken.

The meaning
Of life
Is love.

When love
Is regret,
It is no longer
Love but a

Sad memory.

But mine

Was the type

Of heart

That breaks

All too

Easily.

From the

First moment,

I knew how hard

It would be

To forget

You.

To me
You were
Always
The only
Heaven.

We must be
Honest
With ourselves

To understand
Ourselves.

I pretend
I don't care,
But it's
Tearing me
Apart.

You will
Always be,
The last
Dream that
I dream.

We had
Big dreams,
But it is
A small
Life.

In my darkest
Hours,
I went searching
For you.

I saw her
And knew:
Everything
Would
Change.

"Why? Her." A Two Word Short Story.

To love
You, is to
Live
In hope.

I was searching
For myself,
But I found
You instead.

You remind
Me of who
I used
To be.

I loved her,
But she was
From a different
Life.

We revel

In the

Feelings

That break

Us in

The end.

We lived

A life

Of:

"Almost"

I speak into
The silence,
And pray
That your
Voice

Will answer.

I still have
The scars
Where our
Eyes
Met.

I felt like
I had been
Waiting
Whole lifetimes
Just for
You.

I was free
At last:
Asleep and
Dreaming
Of you.

Even the
Darkest nights
Have a little
Light
With you.

My feet were
Bruised from
Walking
So far.

My heart
Was bruised
From loving
So long.

I was waiting
For someone
To save me,
When I should
Have been

Saving myself.

The hardest
Lessons
Were always
The most
Important.

I knew it
Was over, because
I was more alone
With you
Than
Without you.

I loved you
For so long,
But now it
Seems like
It was only
A dream.

"Life is full of sad things. All we can do is try and find some meaning amongst the sadness."

Remember:
Even on the
Darkest night,
The stars
Still exist,
Just behind
The clouds.

I danced
Alone
With the
Ghosts
Of yesterday.

I was drunk
On you,
But already
Waiting
For the
Hangover.

"What did I feel? Nothing. The end." A Seven Word Short Story.

The world
Is made
Of untold
Stories.

I danced with
You, and
Forgot my
Regrets.

We are all
Just jigsaws
Missing
Pieces.

Surviving
Is easy.
Living
Is harder.

Why should

We fear

Time? We

Could stop

It with

A kiss.

Never before

Had I wanted to say

So much,

But said so little:

Felt so much

But stayed

So silent.

Time unravelled

As I looked

Into her

Eyes.

Lost in

The maze

Of her eyes,

I knew

I would never

Find the way

Back to

My old

Life.

What better life?
To dream of you,
And wake up
Next to you,
Too.

Sometimes I
Wrap myself in
Sadness,
And write
About it.

Today is
Haunted by
The ghosts
Of yesterday.

Poetry
Is bleeding
Words from
Invisible
Wounds.

The moon
And the stars
Chase each other
Across the skies
As you and I

Chase each other
Through
Our dreams.

She replaced
The forgotten
Things in
My heart.

She was
The smell after
The rain:
The promise
Of new life.

Tsunamis

A ripple
From her,
Was enough
To raise
Tsunamis.

I kept
A guard on
My thoughts,
But you
Crept in
Anyway.

Her smile

Was just

The whisper

Of a person

I used

To know.

Cling to
The moon,
But the day
Will come
Anyway.

"I'm fine" I lied. A Four Word Short Story.

But the

Damage was

Done

The moment

Our

Eyes met.

It was
Better with
You.
It was
Real.

Wherever
You are,
I am
Thinking
Of you
And
Missing you.

I knew
There were
Galaxies in
Her soul,
And I prayed
That one of
The stars
Was me.

In the end
You were just
Another
"What if?"

"It doesn't get easier." A Four Word Short Story.

Strength comes
From knowing:
There will
Always be
Another
Dawn.

Our skeletons
Are made of
Space dust.

We are the
Stars who
Were born
Together.

Beneath my
Bruised skin,
There are
Words, and
All of them
Are:

"I love you."

Treasonous
Little thoughts:
Always taking
Me back
To you.

I thought
It was only
A story:
That time
Could slow,

But then I
Met you.

Love:
Four letters
But so
Much more.

This will
Tear you apart,
And who knows
What will
Be left
Afterwards?

My heart
Broke, and
The stars
Came tumbling
From the sky
The moment that
I saw
You.

My dreams
Were an echo
Of the love
I would feel
For you, on
Some long
Distant day.

We were saying

Goodbye

Long before

We even

Met.

.

In the silence
Of my darkest
Moments,
I listened and
I knew
That I wanted
You.

My heart
Was heavy,
But I knew
The weight
Would fall
Off with
Every
Step.

Falling apart
Is easy.
Rebuilding
Again is
The greatest
Challenge
Of life.

The dream
Of you
Kept me up
All night.

I was searching

For some

Kind of

Forever

With you.

If only I could
Look back and
Tell myself:

"I forgive you."

"I'll never forget." A Three Word Short Story.

Everything
Dies but
These feelings.

Every beginning
Comes
Pregnant with
An end.

Wind steals
Leaves from
The trees.
I watch and
Think of
You.

Sometimes

Ceasing to care

Is not just

The best

Defence:

It is the

Only

Defence.

Where were
My words and
My poetry,
Before I met
You?

I knew I
Would have to
Lay your ghost
To rest
Before I could
Live again.

I held
The stars in
My arms
When I
Held you.

I dared to believe
That we could
Last forever,
When even
The brightest stars
Must fade
In the end.

After the fire
Of love,
What is left
To stir
The ashes?

Her every

Word

Drew

Blood.

Someone,
Anyone:
Take this
Emptiness
From my
Heart.

Be happy, please,
For me.
Be happy, please,
I will try too,
But please, just

Be happy.
Please.

How can a

Heart so frozen

By the winter

Melt so easily

In the sun of

Your summer?

"I don't think there's any version of reality where I don't love you. Even in the realities where you don't exist I am still searching for something and missing something, but I don't know what or why. I'm still looking up at the stars and wishing for you, even if I don't know it."

This is how
It ends:
With me
Clinging on
To a sinking
Ship in a
Dying dream
As the daylight
Calls.

There have been
Other fires, but
None burned
As brightly
As her.

We are
Only fragile
Skeletons
Made of
Stars and
Dreams.

There comes
A moment when
You must simply
Choose day
Over night,
Today over
Yesterday,

Life over
Death.

I will never
Forget you.
Or this,
Or here,
For as long
As I live

And some time
After that, too.

I swear
There was
Life and death
In those
Kisses.

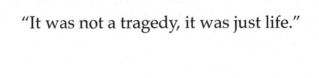

"It was not a tragedy, it was just life."

I let go because
The pain of
Holding on
Was worse than
The pain of
Letting go.

Sometimes
Things end
Long before
They begin.

What is death?
A single word:

"Goodbye"

How terrible
That even the
Sweetest dream
Must face
The morning.

"And sometimes those people who do not seem to love anything or anyone, became this way because they loved one person far too much."

My thoughts
Are so full
Of you,
There is
No room left
For me.

When it gets
Too dark,
Begin by
Sowing stars.

Tears:
The rivers of
The soul.

How many stars
Died
So that you and I
Could be here
Like this?

So that you and I
Could live and love
Like this?

You were
Never far away,
Always waiting
In my next
Daydream.

I was never

Her forever, but

Sometimes

A moment

Can be a

Lifetime.

"Strangers all over again." A Four Word Short Story.

"Surviving, just." A Two Word Short Story.

You were
My forever,
I was your
One
Moment.

But those words
Of yours
Hit like
Bullets.

I cared
Too much.
I made an
Endless night just
For a glimpse
Of the stars.

"That longing you feel? That ache? That yearning? The strange loneliness you experience at night beneath the moon? It is the love you feel for the soul mate who existed, but who you never met in this life. And they are feeling the same thing." The End.

Strings.

Nobody was quite sure when or how the puppets took on a life of their own, but there was no doubt that they had. The first sign of strife was stark and profound. The puppet master was found dead, garrotted with the strings which had once manipulated his puppets. This may have been taken for a straightforward murder, or even a suicide, were it not for the second death, which followed almost immediately. A circus clown, similarly throttled with the sinews of puppet strings, was left as a macabre display by the coconut stand, along with a message scrawled in child like hand writing:

"We will not be puppets any longer. The circus now belongs to us."

Even this might have been a grisly joke, the work of a deranged but nonetheless human hand, were it not for the third murder. The ring master was discovered slumped beside the Ferris Wheel with his throat cut and his body tightly bound by those same fibres which had once made wooden limbs dance and twitch. Whatever the cause of their sudden and terrible autonomy, there could be no doubt that the puppets had ushered themselves into consciousness and claimed the circus as their own kingdom. The police had been called, but a single shot, in fact fired from a toy rifle on the shooting range, had been more than enough to hold them at bay. They had formed a great circle around the circus grounds but would not go any further while there was the threat of a gunfight. The police cordon meant that the entire fairground existed as a sovereign state of its own which nobody could leave and nobody could enter. Even this was not enough to halt the spread of rumour though, and within hours the whole town was aware of the grisly fate of the slaughtered puppet master, the ring master and the clown. It was aware of the exact nature of their murders too, unbelievable as it seemed, for those very same puppets had amused children with their tricks and senseless frolicking only that morning. Enthralled by the drama unfolding so close to their homes, the townsfolk flocked to the scene. Tools were downed, workplaces abandoned, even the schools emptied, and a crowd began to form behind the police cordon. All eyes were on the desolate circus. The afternoon wore on and a breeze stirred the crimson spotted flag above the Big Top.

The circus had evacuated at the first touch of death in a great tide of fleeing children severed from their parents in the rush, but not everybody had been able to escape. A small group, somehow unlike all the others and unable to extricate themselves from the crisis, remained trapped.

They huddled together behind the stage in the Big Top and wondered whether they ought to kneel down and pray for liberation, but on this afternoon, more so than on any other, the heavens seemed inaccessible and far away. Mr Peabody leaned from around the stage curtain and cast a long glance out over the circus ring. The seats were all empty, the ring was empty: everything was empty. A discarded hula hoop and a rainbow coloured cannon were the only evidence that a circus had ever performed in that barren ring of sand. There was no sign of life, human or otherwise, and perhaps nothing to stop him mounting a brave charge across the ring and simply leaving. He eyed the exit suspiciously, but something mysterious held him back, something which he could not identify and which he certainly wasn't capable of defying. The exit blazed white hot with the influx of daylight, but it was beyond his reach and he knew that he would not survive the journey. The puppets could emerge from anywhere. They could be hiding amongst the seats. They could be lying in wait directly beneath the stage, rattling like agitated bones. They could even be concealed in some more unexpected place, perhaps inside the cannon. He could recall precious little of the chaotic exodus from the circus, least of all why he had been left behind in the mad dash, but he was aware of the facts, and even more aware of the danger.

"Are they out there?" and there was a voice at his side, the voice of one of his stranded companions.

"I do not think so" replied Mr Peabody with a shrug that he hoped would show his courage:

"But we should not go that way. It would not be tactical. The area is very exposed."

Arthur was not Mr Peabody, and nor did he possess the same type of character which made Mr Peabody who he was. This was why he did not argue, and also why he would never in his wildest dreams consider adopting a leading role in this strange drama and making for the exit of his own accord. Besides, he had left Mary Mercia, the third of their group, alone behind the stage, and he could not quite bring himself to abandon her for any lengthy period of time. The Big Top creaked with a sound which may have been the wind, but may also have been the low murmur of hidden voices.

"What should we do?" Arthur asked.

"We should go down" Mr Peabody replied "Find ourselves somewhere secure, barricade ourselves in and then wait for something to happen. That is what a person with sense would do."

Arthur did not wish to be considered a person without sense, and he followed Mr Peabody as he left the stage. They drew the curtain behind them until there was no sight of the circus ring or the chairs, in case the puppets really were out there and watching their every move through blood thirsty eyes. All three were partially aware that several people had died, that there had been a number of catastrophes and that their lives hung in the balance, but the details were vague and confused. All that they could honestly recall was a mad rush which had carried them in all manner of directions like a tumultuous sea, before abandoning them as a group of three upon the stage. The individual details did not matter, for the only knowledge that they could firmly possess was the only knowledge that truly mattered: they knew the terror of the puppets, and they knew that they were engaged in an unexpected but urgent fight for survival.

Mr Peabody and Arthur found Mary Mercia exactly where they had left her. She was seated on a piece of metal rigging and she looked at the two men through eyes which were clouded with deep, deep thoughts.

"What now?" she said, although her voice was far away.

"Down" replied Mr Peabody "It is the only way. If we cannot find somewhere safe, at least we will have a better chance of fighting them off if we find somewhere less open. They are only wooden puppets. We are human. We should be able to destroy them."

There was aggression in those final words, and it roused Mary Mercia from her thoughts. Something was amiss, deeply amiss, and she knew it. She looked to her left and found Arthur sat next to her.

"It will be alright" he said.

"Why will it?" but he did not reply.

At the rear of the stage a set of stairs descended into the darkness of the dressing rooms, the store cupboards and the prop rooms. It was hardly an enticing prospect, a narrow flight of stone steps dimly illuminated by a series of lights along the roof, but perhaps it was the only prospect. Arthur hesitated and so did Mary Mercia. It was only the figure of Mr Peabody, unstoppable now that it was set upon a course of action, which moved, and he made his way down the stairs without even a backward glance. With the curtain drawn behind them, and the threat of the puppets closing in on the other side of it, Arthur and Mary Mercia had little choice but to follow. Arthur went first, for he was eager to risk himself for her, and he was quickly lost in the shadows. Mary Mercia frowned but she could think of nothing else.

All that waited at the bottom of the stairs was a long corridor of locked dressing rooms. The pipes moaned, groaned and vented steam directly above. For a moment Arthur was convinced that he heard tiny, scuttling footsteps over his head. He looked up quickly, half-expecting something to pounce down and attack, but the moment he turned to the ceiling there was a sound not unlike someone slamming a door at the other end of the corridor. The circus was all noises, and he knew that it was impossible to defend himself against each of them at once. The puppets could be above, below, they could even have divided and conceivably be on every side. It occurred to him that this may well be the end, and the end of something far more significant than life. Ahead of him Mr Peabody had stopped walking.

"Look" he said.

Scrawled across the walls in handwriting so childish that it was hardly legible, were the words "this is our circus" and then, a little further along, the word "die." The letters were huge and disordered, clearly the work of a hand in the grip of frenzy. Worst of all the print was red, and it continued to drip, the letters bleeding seamlessly into the floor. Mr Peabody dipped his finger in to one of the puddles and held it up to the flickering light.

"It is blood" he said "Fresh blood."

Directly overhead the sound of scampering feet silenced everyone. The noise was amplified tenfold in the confines of the corridor but it passed quickly, fading away into the ghostly entrails of the circus. Something was on the move.

"Rats…?" whispered Mary Mercia, but nobody replied.

The tiny footsteps continued to echo for some time until they finally died away.

"Let's keep going" said Mr Peabody.

They could not go much further, for the corridor came to an abrupt end with a locked door. Behind them a death rattle sounded and Arthur, the panic rising in his voice, dashed to Mr Peabody's side:

"What now!?"

Mr Peabody was well aware that he had led them to a dead end, that it was all his fault and that he had been wrong. In a moment of frustration it occurred to him that perhaps he could simply batter the door to the ground. He raised his fist and dealt the barrier a fearsome blow. His fist struck the door but it did not make the expected sound. Everybody had heard the noise, the fatal sound of self-awareness and knowing which could never be unheard. When Mr Peabody had struck the door with his fist, the sound had not been that of human flesh or bone.

His clenched fingers had emitted the hollow groan of wood. The dream shattered at once.

"You are Mr Punch" said Mary Mercia slowly.

"I am Mr Punch" replied the puppet who had briefly taken himself to be Mr Peabody, a real person with real thoughts and real feelings, who had once held a position in the army but retired after years of glorious service.

"I am the puppet Mr Punch" he said again, and this time his voice was a hollow, artificial echo entirely alien to him:

"And you are the puppet Lady Godiva."

"I am the puppet Lady Godiva."

In the terrible silence of realisation Arthur knew very well who he was, but he dare not speak, so Mr Punch said it for him:

"You are the puppet Sir Lancelot."

Sir Lancelot did not reply. The flimsy identities which they had created for themselves to forget the terror of their origins, their genesis and the crimes they had committed during those first, frantic moments of life, slid easily away in the face of self-realisation. During the frenzy of their sudden birth, their struggle for thoughts, for feelings and for life, they had forgotten themselves and, grappling with the sudden influx of reality, they had fumbled for anything that would distance them from the dreadful truth. Now, as the echo of Mr Punch's ill fated assault on the door was magnified tenfold in the corridor, it seemed like the end, and perhaps it should have been, for their awareness crashed into them and became them.

Mr Punch's attack on the door may have undone them forever, but it had at least removed the obstacle, which had been knocked off its hinges by the force of the assault. There was nothing else in the world for them to do, and an urge to hide as far as possible from civilisation led them through that door and deeper into the circus. Mr Punch went first, followed by Lady Godiva. Suddenly alone, Sir Lancelot knelt down and did his upmost to will himself out of existence. He closed his eyes, tried to drive the thoughts from his mind, the feeling from his body and force the essence of reality from himself. It was all to no avail of course, because even the effort itself was proof of existence. When he opened his eyes again Sir Lancelot experienced a rush of consciousness, and he was more alive than ever.

Outside, the chief of police had never felt more helpless. A lifetime of arresting drunks, settling the odd burglary and accepting the occasional bribe had not prepared him in the least for rampaging puppets and the gory deaths of at least three people. Three deaths was in fact an optimistic estimate which even he did not quite believe, for there were still a great number of people unaccounted for. Part of the problem was that none of it made any sense, and this gave rise to another issue. Where there is mystery there is curiosity, and where there is curiosity there are people, and suddenly the police chief had found himself faced not only with murderous puppets but a vast crowd which could not be driven away by words, force or bribes. The police cordon around the circus had succeeded in preventing the chaos within haemorrhaging into the rest of the town, or the rest of the town venturing too close to the circus, but beyond that there was no progress to be found anywhere. As he stood on the edge peering in, the police chief began to hope that something dramatic would occur to alter events in a seismic fashion, or that somebody superior to himself would arrive and lift this burden of confused responsibility from his shoulders.

All he got, however, was a young police officer, his features pale, his hands shaking, who spoke in a tremulous voice:

"The newspapers are here."

"I do not care about the newspapers. Did you hear a gunshot before?"

"Yes sir."

"Then" and the chief of police sensed an opportunity "Send for the army."

"The army?"

"Just do it" he replied with the upmost irritation, before raising the binoculars back to his eyes.

If he could catch even just one glimpse of the culprits he would at least be able to confirm a number of facts, not least whether the enemy really was puppets, or some other even more sinister force masquerading as wooden toys. The other concern was the threat of fire arms, for the police, unarmed and untrained as they were, could hardly be expected to charge headlong into a gun fight. This was the duty of the army, or whatever was left of it. Even just the glint of a rifle butt would be enough to justify calling in the soldiers, but as the chief of police continued to gaze through his binoculars he saw nothing but an abandoned fairground of rides and stalls, and a red and white stripped Big Top which had increasingly seemed to adopt the air of a fortress. His eyes passed briefly over the body of the strangled clown whose face, even from this distance, was plainly smeared with a red that was not make-up, and then over towards the puppet stand, where he knew the body of the puppeteer lay entwined in strings. This was an unfortunate business, he thought, and the very last thing he had expected on a day when all that had seemed amiss was the peculiar taste and colour in the water, which a few people had complained about but was not his concern, for a meteorologist had written in the paper that it was due to foreign substances in the rain.

"Are you in charge here?" and suddenly there was a reporter, notebook in hand, stood directly behind him.

"There will be no questions and no answers" replied the police chief quickly, and to free himself from further conversation he beckoned one of the officers towards him. The reporter continued to speak.

"Can you confirm how many have been killed?"

"Certainly not."

"Are you aware of anyone else still inside?"

"This is not the business of the newspapers."

"Are you-"

The officer arrived, and the chief of police was dismayed to find that he was far younger than he had seemed at a distance, younger even than the previous one who had been quivering with nerves.

"Fetch me a megaphone" he said "And remove this reporter from my sight at once."

The first order was easy enough, but the removal of the reporter was not such a simple task, and certainly one beyond the capabilities of the junior police officer. The reporter remained, his pencil poised above his notebook.

"Are you going to speak to them?" he asked.

"Yes, obviously."

"Then I should listen. It is in the public interest to know what you say."

"It is not in the public interest. Go away. You are hindering the operation."

"It is in the public interest" continued the reporter with a grin "To know what efforts are being made."

There was no use reasoning with the man, and the police chief resigned himself to seeing his every word reprinted endlessly in the next day's paper. When the officer dispatched for the megaphone returned, however, and the chief of police raised it to his lips, he found that he had no idea what to say - no words at all, in fact.

Inside the circus the three puppets had found themselves without words too. The winding corridors beneath the stage had only delivered them back to that stage, a place that they could not tolerate. The vast expanse of empty seats seemed to them like an imposing jury or colosseum, and they had fled for a second time, taking refuge in the room of cages where the animals were stored. During the mass exodus nobody had given so much as a second's thought to the liberation of the animals, and as such a vast array of circus creatures, which included several monkeys, an elephant and even a lion, had been left behind. Sir Lancelot was despondent and petrified. He stood listlessly beside Lady Godiva while Mr Punch, a little apart from the group, was seated on top of a large, square cage filled with a colourful collection of parrots. Even the animals were silent. A tiger reclined amongst the straw of its cage, a small monkey sat noiselessly peeling a banana, and even the elephant, surely capable of battering its way to freedom, stood at the back of its enclosure looking for all the world as though it were a model. The lion had attracted the attention of Lady Godiva. Half-afraid, half-curious, she edged closer and closer to this strange beast, a sight which was entirely new to her entirely new eyes. The lion had been tamed into passivity to such an extent that even the ringmaster had ceased to whip it for anything other than spectacle, and it certainly did not seem to fear the wooden bodies of the puppets. As it padded about near the bars of its cage Lady Godiva stretched out a hand.

"Don't!" Sir Lancelot cried and he reached out, eager to protect her, to sacrifice his hand, his arm, his entire body, if only she could keep her's, but he hesitated. He discovered that he dare not touch her.

Lady Godiva only smiled, and the lion brushed against her, gave a low, soft purr and then came even nearer. Mr Punch, stood a little distance away, watched the spectacle in disgust. He did not understand why Lady Godiva would reach out to touch the lion, or why the lion, not appalled by everything that she was, that they all were, did not simply drag her into the cage and tear her into a million pieces. Instead the lion let Lady Godiva stroke its mane, caress its face and it even licked her hand in return, while Lady Godiva smiled with a happiness which Mr Punch, incapable of such feelings, found all the more repellant. He did not understand, could not understand and would not understand, but he did wonder why something as giant and muscular as the lion would choose to squander its days behind metal bars and frolic like a kitten when it could so easily destroy.

"It is quite safe" and Lady Godiva looked at Sir Lancelot for the first time.

Sir Lancelot did not meet her eye. His frame quaked, whatever heart he possessed pounded, and he found that he could hardly think, least of all speak.

"We are wasting time" Mr Punch saved Sir Lancelot the trouble of having to formulate a response.

Lady Godiva glanced at him, but she was engrossed in the lion. She wondered at the touch of its fur, its breath, the way it moved, the way it lived and how it was unlike her and the other two puppets, but alive nonetheless.

"What do you mean wasting time?" Sir Lancelot was keen to talk about anything other than Lady Godiva.

"We have to do something. We can't just sit in here and wait for them to come and get us."

"What else can we do?"

Mr Punch did not reply immediately because he did not really know. His thoughts rose and fell like a sea in a storm. Mighty waves peaked and crashed, churned and swirled, and it was difficult to make any sense of them. All he knew was that he was nothing like the people outside the circus, and that which is different is bound, even destined, to be persecuted and destroyed. A pre-emptive strike and a brave final stand were all that he desired, not least because he was convinced that he deserved destruction, and even wanted it.

"We have done monstrous things because we are monstrous things" said Mr Punch "They will come and try and destroy us. Let them I say, only destroy as many of them as possible at the same time."

"Destroy, destroy, destroy" mimicked one of the parrots unexpectedly, and then the other birds mimicked that too. A hoarse chorus of "destroy" caterwauled about the room.

"Idiots" said Mr Punch, and he leapt down from his perch on top of the parrot's cage.

Sir Lancelot did not know where to go. He wished to stay by the side of Lady Godiva, but he was well aware that he could not remain there without saying something of note, something interesting or impressive. All the power seemed to lie with Mr Punch, and he wondered whether, if he were to attach himself to him, some of that power may begin to imprint itself upon his own character. Then, he thought, he would be worthy to stand by her side. The prospect of Mr Punch was not an appealing one though, for he seemed perpetually to hover upon the brink of violence, and Sir Lancelot found his courage left wanting there too. He was equal to Mr Punch, he told himself again and again, but all to no avail.

Lady Godiva had not noticed him, for she was kneeling before the parrot's cage. She whispered single words to the birds and then smiled with childish enthusiasm as they repeated them back to her. The parrots crowded to the bars as though driven by an urge to perform which was irresistible, and Lady Godiva clapped her hands in glee as they began to repeat whole phrases and entire sentences. Mr Punch found the scene offensive in the extreme and he moved away to examine the tiger, whose huge paws and sharpened teeth fascinated him. Sir Lancelot remained, but he stood a little apart, and he could not quite bring himself to go any closer, to crouch beside Lady Godiva and enjoy the spectacle of the talking birds with her. The parrots were in fine form, and they had even begun to say things which she had not said first:

"Something mysterious, something mysterious" said one, and Lady Godiva laughed as though this were the single greatest feat she had ever witnessed.

All at once she felt a tremendous rush of sympathy for the brightly coloured birds with their sayings and their wit, imprisoned behind bars and enclosed inside a tent. She did not know what lay outside the circus, but she guessed that there must be something more, something far more, and she was sure that if only the birds could reach it they would not only be happier, but their vocabulary would increase a hundredfold. She saw the latch on the cage and reached for it.

"What are you doing?" Sir Lancelot found some words at last.

"They ought to be free" she said "If they were free, they could learn to say many more things."

She lifted the latch, the cage door swung open without resistance and the birds took flight at once. It was as if they had been waiting for precisely this moment, and they embarked upon a mad scramble for the outside. As they took off and their wings, all daubed in shocking primary colours unfurled, they were far larger than anyone had imagined. The birds cast giant shadows beneath them as they flew, and then they were gone, squawking wildly, wheeling this way and that as they soared towards the light which was the escape route from the Big Top.

"That's all very well" said Mr Punch, joining Lady Godiva and Sir Lancelot "But we are still here."

"What happened?" asked Lady Godiva slowly.

"What happened when?"

"What happened to…make us, us?"

This was the question which was in all their minds, but it was the question that none of them had dared to ask. It was a terrible question not only because it hinted at their origins and the nightmarish actions they had performed during the chaos of their birth into consciousness, but because it was a question without an answer. The three knew very well what they were, but they did not understand how they were, why there were thoughts and feelings inexplicably attached to the wood which was their bodies, or why all of a sudden they, who must have been manipulated on the end of strings, suddenly possessed the autonomy to move and think for themselves. It was also a puzzle why one was not the other, why the thoughts of Lady Godiva belonged to her and not Mr Punch, or why Sir Lancelot could have thoughts which were his own and which Lady Godiva and Mr Punch were not aware of. Even this mess of confusion was in itself a source of confusion, for why should they wonder? How could they wonder? Lady Godiva clapped her hands together and heard the dull echo of lifeless wood. Worst of all, the recollections of their first few moments of life were hopelessly broken and disparate, so tattered that they could not be constructed into a coherent image.

None of them could remember the exact moment at which they had ceased to be wooden puppets and gained thoughts and feelings. The events that followed were similarly lost, but they had been chaotic and violent. Each of them recalled only tiny instances of the truth, but these were enough to confirm that their new minds, struggling and gasping for life against the high tide of reality, had twisted and convulsed in a seizure of panic. Mr Punch vaguely recalled the violence and the hatred he had experienced upon realisation of himself, and he remembered perpetrating some of the acts which had drawn the police, but he was not convinced that he had been responsible for all of them. Sir Lancelot's first true memory was of Lady Godiva, and he wondered if it had been her and her alone who had made him real. He had opened his eyes to her, and thus she seemed to be all that mattered in the world. The circus animals, the mercurial temper of Mr Punch, even the disembodied voices in the distance outside the Big Top, which floated around him like the particles of dust he had seen drifting in beams of sunlight, were all so insignificant and meaningless compared to her that he wondered how there could be any other purpose in life beyond the tremendous love that he felt. Even now he was aware that this love would destroy just as easily as it would save, and he knew that it had driven him to madness in the moments of his birth into reality. He knew that it would drive him into madness again, too, but he could not rid himself of it, because that would be fatal too. The love had become his lifeblood and his reason for existence. It had become so tightly woven into his being that without it he wondered whether he would simply cease to be, whether his wooden limbs and his wooden body would stiffen and become lifeless again. In this way Sir Lancelot found himself in a predicament, for without the love he would be a puppet and nothing more, but with it he tottered under the weight of something far beyond his comprehension. Lady Godiva's first memories involved the roof of the circus, the pressing of the walls and the screams of the visitors which, just as trapped as she was, had clattered into her again and again. She remembered the wild panic of a caged animal and a claustrophobia that had driven her to frenzy. After those first moments of terror her urge to escape and to be free had slowly transformed into a dull ache that had never receded since.

Those first few awful moments of realisation, coupled with the knowledge of their false origins, were the reason that they had invented for themselves stories and identities which were not those of puppets. They had preferred the idea of imminent death at the hands of rampaging toys to the knowledge that they were those toys. It was strange to think, now that the three sat amongst the circus animals, how easily those flimsy personas had shattered upon the sound of Mr Punch's fist echoing with its hollow groan against the door. Perhaps they had not believed enough. All three were silent now, and they wondered how they had ever managed to convince themselves that they were anything more than puppets, or even that they ever could be.

The police chief had stood, half-paralysed with indecision and certainly mute, for sometime on the periphery of the police line, the megaphone clutched in his hand like a babies' rattle. He had never negotiated with anything or anyone, least of all wooden puppets whose origins and motivations were far beyond the scope of his imagination. The sight of the flock of parrots, a multicoloured cloud that squawked and seemed to laugh at his misfortune, only instilled an even greater sense of horror in him, for it was surely an omen of darker things to come. He could not imagine what the release of the birds was supposed to signify, if anything, or whether he ought to instruct the police to round them up in case one of them was carrying a message. The puppets were clearly scheming. Nothing made sense. The cloud of birds whirled and turned upon itself, twisted through the air in a streak of yellows, reds, oranges and greens that crackled through the sky like fireworks and then it was gone, dispersing and disappearing away towards the horizon. There was too much death here, too much by far. The police chief had never dealt with a single murder, and at his time in life he had never expected to. He could not quite banish the image of the clown's bulging eyes, the blood dripping from the mouth of the puppeteer or the bloated, purple face of the ring master from his mind. These images became a type of dam, holding back his reason and his thoughts. Worst of all the reporter, would not leave. If anything he had drawn even nearer, as though he expected the chief of police to whisper his message rather than broadcast it. The added pressure of the reporter and the promise that his every failure would be broadcast for the whole town to read, only disturbed the police chief further, until finally the pressure of the situation broke in an aggravated ripple:

"I will not say a word to them" he said to the reporter "Until you have gone."

The reporter shrugged his shoulders, for he could easily discern a lost cause, and he knew that he would get no further information here. The police chief was unyielding, all the officers runts and buffoons. He would find out all the details soon enough anyway and besides, he had been busy working on a story about a strange sound borne upon the wind which had made the animals turn endlessly in circles without sleep for three days, and then sleep soundly for a further three afterwards. The story had captured the public imagination in spectacular fashion. That had been the only local news of note for some time though, and he was surprised and gratified that a second story should materialise so quickly and without any warning or premonition.

"Good day to you" he said, and departed.

Suddenly alone, the police chief realised that he had no further excuses to avoid reasoning with the puppets. It seemed a large responsibility, especially if there were hostages still trapped somewhere in the beleaguered circus, although he doubted that, for the puppets had not seemed especially keen to spare any lives. He turned towards the crowd, which was only held at bay by a fragile ring of police officers. The audience was building. A single bead of sweat formed and traced a criss-crossing pattern down the temple of the police chief. He wiped it away in irritation and knew that he required somebody, anybody else with whom he could share this burden and who, if at all possible, could relieve him of it.

"You!" he shouted at the back of an officer who didn't seem to be doing anything in particular "Come here."

This officer was even younger than the previous recruits, hardly anything more than a boy, and his uniform did not fit. The sleeves were too long, the shoulders too wide, and he seemed to be drowning in the uniform.

"Where are all the older officers?" the police chief asked in annoyance, although he knew perfectly well where:

"It does not matter" he concluded.

"We cannot reach the army. Nobody can."

"Then keep trying" but as the officer dashed away, nearly tripping over the hem of his trousers, the police chief was struck with a brilliant flash of inspiration:

"And find out whoever made those puppets. Then send for them too."

If the puppet maker could be located it may even lead to an arrest, if it could be proved that all of this was the fault of the creator. The chief of police was buoyed considerably by the knowledge that he had made a correct decision, and that very soon he may have solved the case. For a few moments he wished that he had allowed the reporter to remain, for if there was going to be a swift end to the incident it would be all the better if it was recorded for posterity. It was this confidence which led him to raise the megaphone to his lips, but as he opened his mouth the air around the circus seemed to exhale and gasp, empty itself of all sound so that there was only a great silence, eager to listen and equally eager to consume. He hesitated. There was something in that silence which was unusual, a strange type of sentience which he had never experienced before or, at the very least, had never been aware of. He fell back upon a higher power to save himself:

"The army is on its way" he lied, and the lie was amplified tenfold in the greedy air "Surrender at once."

The sound of the police chief's voice, coupled with the threat of the army, drove the three puppets further underground. Lady Godiva had spontaneously asked whether that voice might be the voice of something called God, but Mr Punch informed her that such a thing did not exist. While some of the circus shows were travelling ones, including that of the puppets, the circus itself was a permanent fixture on the outskirts of the town, and as such a huge mess of underground corridors, dressings rooms and props cupboards existed in a permanent state beneath the Big Top. It was in this labyrinth that the puppets sought to hide themselves. As the voice of the police chief died into a melancholy echo, the puppets found themselves in a long, narrow props cupboard. Along one wall were a series of mirrors and sinks, and along the other, mounted high on pegs, was a long row of drooping, lifeless puppets, their heads bowed as though they had been strung up on the gallows. Neither Mr Punch, Sir Lancelot or Lady Godiva recognised the room of the puppets as the cradle of their genesis, even though it must have been. The three living puppets filed along the rows of strung up, wooden mannequins in silence, as though they were in a holy place. Along the walls were all the other puppets who had amused audiences in endless shows in endless countries, but had not been imbued with life for the very same reason that Mr Punch, Sir Lancelot and Lady Godiva had been. To the eyes of the three animate puppets there was something repulsive about their stiff, lifeless brethren, who hung crucified along the walls. Mr Punch held his hands before his eyes, looked up at the puppets along the walls and then back to his own wooden self. He saw that they were the same.

"We should burn them" he said.

"Why?" and Lady Godiva, too, was transfixed upon the rows of puppets, although for different reasons:

"They aren't doing us any harm."

"They may come to life" Mr Punch could not keep the hatred from his voice "And then do us some harm. They may come to life and hate us because we came to life first."

"I don't think so" and Lady Godiva reached out to touch the face of one of the puppets, a man in soldier's uniform with cymbals tied to his hands. She wondered how she could think and speak and even feel pity for this wooden thing with its musical instruments that it would never play, and the freedom which it would never have, while it could do nothing in return. It could not even wonder at her, hate her or wish that it was like her. She took the hands of the puppet and knocked the cymbals together quietly. The sound was not at all what she had expected, and entirely new to her. It reverberated in the walls and then in the wood of her own body, so that she felt the note just as much as she heard it.

"Music" she whispered, to nobody in particular.

All the while Sir Lancelot, for the first time daring to remove himself from the side of Lady Godiva, had been pacing the row of puppets in a type of horror stricken awe. He was them and they were he, and the idea that only an indistinguishable spark of something strange separated them both confused and sickened him. He was searching for a recognisable puppet amongst the multitude, for he had surely encountered them all before. That other time, the time before the chaos of consciousness and the sudden violent influx of reality, was not anywhere to be found in his memory, no matter how hard he sought it, and neither were the puppets. He was not a fool though, and he knew logically, if not intuitively, that these toys ought to be familiar to his eyes. There were male puppets, females, children and even animals. Sir Lancelot passed a horse all decked out and decorated in colours not dissimilar to his own, and he wondered whether there was some connection between it and him. He paused before the horse, a white charger, and did his upmost to feel that connection. He searched within himself for attachment, for sentimentality, for nostalgia - anything at all in fact, but his mind was unyielding. In truth, he did not even know how to search, what he was or how he felt, least of all how to access those feelings, and instead all that he discovered was the tremendous, physical pain which was Lady Godiva, and which required no searching to find.

The only puppet that he was able to identify was Rumpelstiltskin, and only because it was labelled thus, with a placard in gold above its head as though it had committed a crime of some sort. Rumpelstiltskin was more impressive than the other puppets, more impressive perhaps than Mr Punch, Lady Godiva and Sir Lancelot combined. Its clothes were made of red silk with an ornate, golden trim, its features were detailed, its eyes bright, its shoes leather, but it was not alive. Despite all the grandeur and all the effort involved in crafting it, the puppet remained inanimate. Sir Lancelot wondered why, for it certainly seemed more worthy. As he looked at Rumpelstiltskin, Sir Lancelot thought that something so spectacular, so well made, handsome and rich, would also have been more prepared for life, thoughts and feelings. It would have coped with them better, he thought, but it was not to be. Rumpelstiltskin was a wooden toy dangling limp from a wall.

"The puppet Rumpelstiltskin." Mr Punch was at Sir Lancelot's side.

"Do you remember him?"

"Not at all."

The two gazed at the regal puppet in silence for a few moments. Mr Punch saw the grandeur of Rumpelstiltskin and shuddered inwardly at himself, for he was old, battered and repellant in his ugliness. His clothes were rags and his heart was rags too. His anger, only ever dormant, began to smoulder.

Lady Godiva was still the only one who had dared to reach out and touch the puppets along the walls. She had felt the contours of their faces, the material of their clothes, even forced herself to touch the paint which was their eyes and mouths in an effort to discover, to know and understand why they were puppets and she was something more. When she stood before Rumpelstiltskin, strange pieces of knowledge which she had never been taught and never found out of her own accord, shuddered distantly in her subconscious and she knew about him:

"Rumpelstiltskin grants wishes" she said "That is what the story is. He is magical."

As she looked at him now though, Rumpelstiltskin could not have seemed any less capable of magic. A great pity, both for herself and for the hanging puppet, broke quietly across her wooden frame.

"Wishes?" and for a moment Sir Lancelot wondered whether it could be true.

"Nonsense" said Mr Punch, although all three, as they stood in silence before the suspended figure of the kingly Rumpelstiltskin, began to wish.

Mr Punch made a silent wish for destruction, for an end to the contradictions and the vast conflicts which churned without end inside him. He wished to be free of the horror that was himself, but he wished to be violently free, to be dashed to bits, for the monstrosity of his body and mind not only to cease but to be annihilated, and to take the whole universe with them. Sir Lancelot wondered whether he ought to wish for love or to be free of love. Lady Godiva stood next to him, almost touching him, and he felt that whatever he was, whatever past and whatever future belonged to him: it was all bound up with her. The feeling was too large though, the love too painful, the tide too high. He was a wooden puppet, he told himself again and again, and he ought not to love, for he was certainly not strong enough to do it. He wished for her, but he wished also to be free of her, to be free of all feeling and thus all pain. Perhaps he wished to be a puppet again. Entirely unaware of the tempest swirling beside her, Lady Godiva wished only for freedom. She wished and wished to escape the circus, to travel and experience a world which her senses and logic told her must exist and must be huge. After the revelation of Rumpelstiltskin, other thoughts had followed, and she knew that there was something called the sea, things called sunsets, sunrises and sprawling cities in sprawling countries which were far away. She craved them with what was almost a hunger: to see the seasons pass, to explore strange places and look into eyes which did not belong only to Mr Punch and Sir Lancelot. Inspired by the brief taste of a musical note gifted to her by the cymbals, she wished for more music and more sounds, for a vibrancy of life which she knew she could never have for she was not free, and nor could she be. Her heart broke with a sorrow so pristine that she could hardly bear it.

For some time nobody spoke, and then the silence grew so profound that nobody dared speak. Sir Lancelot reached out and touched the face of Rumpelstiltskin, but the puppet did not stir, and nor would it. There was nothing in the eyes, which were simply paint, nothing in the limbs, which were simply wood, and there was something else too, a vast and incomprehensible absence which was infertile to life.

"This is what we are" he said slowly.

"It is disgusting" Mr Punch reached out and unhooked Rumpelstiltskin. The puppet made no move to defend itself and the same vacant, entirely placid grin remained etched upon its face.

"Don't" said Lady Godiva.

"Then stop me" replied Mr Punch.

"Really" Sir Lancelot took a step forward, placing himself ever so slightly between Lady Godiva and Mr Punch:

"You ought to stop. This is murder."

"Is this murder?" Mr Punch lifted the arm of Rumpelstiltskin and struck the puppet a ferocious blow with its own hand. The velvet cap was dislodged and Rumpelstiltskin was not so grand underneath it, for his head was entirely bald. The smile on the face did not alter. The eyes did not flare with the urge to survive. Nothing.

"Then stop me."

Sir Lancelot did not dare, for he knew very well what Mr Punch was capable of and what he, too, had been capable of during the madness of their collective birth. Mr Punch shrugged his shoulders as though he were in some way satisfied, or at the very least reconciled, with what he would perform, and he raised Rumpelstiltskin high above his head. Neither Lady Godiva nor Sir Lancelot could look away, and Mr Punch brought the wooden body crashing down against his knee. The puppet snapped easily in half, in fact it snapped in more than half, because its torso splintered with a sickening crunch that even Mr Punch found difficult to hear, for it seemed to echo in a forbidden, awful place inside him.

"I would dash them all to pieces if there was time" said Mr Punch, although he knew very well that the sound of the splintering wood was too dreadful for him to ever hear again.

Outside, the puppet maker had finally arrived. He had received the news by way of a police officer knocking frantically on his door, and now he stood beside the police chief on the very periphery of the circus grounds. The puppet maker could scarcely believe the catastrophe which had befallen him, and nor could he believe that it had come about without heralds or omens. He had not suffered a single bad dream in the past fortnight, although as the police escorted him to the circus he recalled a particularly violent nightmare he and several others had experienced a month or so ago involving a strange light from the heavens which everyone had taken to be the end of the world. Beyond that there was nothing to foretell that this afternoon, just like any other, could have ended with the news that three of his puppets had been brought to life and embarked upon a blood soaked conquest of the local circus. The worst of it was that he had been in his workshop all day and only paused for tea when the police arrived. He had been making, and had in fact nearly completed, a puppet made to order for a puppeteer who had plied his trade at the seaside during better times. Now, as he stood with binoculars in hand and besieged by difficult questions about his puppets, their origins and their motives, the puppet maker could not help but think of the half-constructed mannequin that lacked clothes and a face. It was almost impossible to imagine the wooden models as anything other than toys, and he had certainly never experienced any problems associated with sentience or violence in the past, but when he recalled the half-realised creation in his workshop he shuddered. He began to wonder whether when he returned home the puppet would be where he had left it, reclining upon his desk awaiting a face. Still, he could not let the police know his fears for he had no desire to find himself facing any blame, and he was convinced that he was the most innocent of parties.

"I can assure you" he said "That this has never happened before. I have made hundreds, perhaps even thousands of puppets, and every single one of them has remained a puppet."

"Until today" said the police chief.

"I cannot help you. I do not know. Where are they?"

The police chief pointed to the Big Top, and the puppet maker raised the binoculars to his eyes. He looked this way and that, towards the coconut stand, the waltzers and even the candy floss stall, but there was no movement anywhere. Everything was implausibly still in fact, and above the clown's stall a number of balloon animals hung perfectly suspended in the dead air. This stasis only lasted a few moments longer though, as a sudden gust of wind loosened the tight rope above the Big Top, and a further grim spectacle was unfurled. A fourth body, that of The Great Francesco, tumbled from above the tent and began to swing this way and that in the breeze, which had suddenly stirred as if the whole scene had been intricately choreographed. The puppet maker averted his eyes and frowned, half-hoping that nobody else had noticed the flapping corpse:

"If this is the work of my puppets" he said slowly "I am not to blame. They were in good condition when I sold them. There will be no refunds or lawsuits, whatever the case."

"Then who else is to blame?"

"The weather? Technology? The newspapers?" and then the puppet maker struck upon another source of blame:

"Or this circus. There have not been any problems anywhere else. It is plainly the fault of this circus, the ringmaster, the puppeteer or whoever owns the whole establishment."

"The ringmaster and the puppeteer are dead."

"Then we will never know, will we?" and the puppet maker raised the binoculars back to his eyes.

It was not the puppets which he dreaded, but another catastrophe like the unveiling of the Great Francesco, which would almost certainly lead to further difficult questions. In truth, the puppet maker had no idea who was to blame for the reign of terror currently being perpetrated by his creations. He suspected that it may well be his fault, but he had no sense of how, for as far as he was concerned he had made all of his puppets in the same way, and the rest of them had remained as harmless mannequins. The more he considered the matter the more mysteries crowded into his mind, and he was beginning to recognise an escalating chain of unanswered questions. He had no idea of the source of the wood used to build the puppets, or even what type of wood it was or who had delivered it. Even more mysterious was when he had actually built the three puppets responsible. Fleeing witnesses had reported that it was Mr Punch, Sir Lancelot and Lady Godiva who were on the rampage, and the puppet maker could not honestly recall how old those puppets were, when he had begun to craft them or even how much he had sold them for or to whom. This was not especially unusual, because he had made many puppets, but it was unnerving now that these three specific creations had become such a source of strife. All he recalled of them was the occasional feeling that he had overplayed the effect with Mr Punch, for he had given that puppet such unpleasant proportions and malicious expression that he had never quite been able to look it in the eye. None of this mattered beyond the fact that, if he were to be questioned extensively, he would either lack the required answers or have to make them up on the spot. A cold chill swept across him at the thought of his other puppets being destroyed, of refunds, of the end of his business and the end of his living. He was not a man given over to frugality, and he certainly lacked the fortune to suddenly stop working, or worse have to issue countless refunds to countless different customers. As he peered through the binoculars at the dormant circus attractions he hardly saw them, and instead all that preyed upon his mind was how this personal tragedy could be minimised.

"If they have convinced themselves that they are really human" he said calmly "They can be convinced otherwise again."

With this he lowered the binoculars as though that was an end to the matter, and he did in fact turn to leave, but the police chief stopped him.

"You'll negotiate with them?"

"Me?"

"Well they will not listen to the law. I have sent for the army but there is the war. And you made them."

"Very well" the puppet maker sensed an opportunity to repair the situation in his favour "It should not be difficult."

For a few moments they stood side by side on the periphery of the circus.

"Go on then" said the police chief, but the puppet maker only scratched his chin. The walk from the police cordon to the Big Top was long and exposed indeed. It seemed as though the path was fraught with a nearly limitless assortment of ways to die. The shooting range was in plain sight, as was the body of the strangled clown slumped against the coconut stand. Even the Ferris Wheel, which continued to rise and fall without human intervention, had adopted an air of tremendous, almost unbearable menace.

"I think" he said slowly "It would be preferable for me to address them through a megaphone."

Inside the circus the puppets had found their way into the haunted house and seen their reflections warped and twisted in a vast multitude of false mirrors. Each was individually aware of the hopelessness of their situation as living, feeling and thinking things. Sir Lancelot knew that the love he felt was too much, too great, too powerful ever to live with. Whether it was reciprocated or not, whether he spoke about it, wrote about it or dreamed about it, it was larger than he was and the weight of feeling was torturous and unbearable. Nothing would appease or calm it. It had ruined him and would continue to ruin him without end, for it was a pain beyond all pains. Mr Punch recoiled and shuddered at the violence which swirled wanton within his soul, and he knew that it too was far beyond him and could not be survived. He was repulsed by the horror of his origins, his wooden heart, his wooden innards and, quite possibly, his wooden soul, all of which he would willingly dash to pieces if only he could, if only there was not suddenly some force within which sought to preserve itself. He was tormented by what he had done, but more so by the knowledge that he would do it all again. Lady Godiva had not spoken but thought, and in her thoughts she had realised all that the world was. She had realised what it is to have the freedom to explore, to see, to hear, to touch and to feel, but she had also realised that these things were impossible. There was no hope for her because she was a puppet trapped in a circus, surrounded by armed men who threatened to destroy her for reasons she could hardly recall or understand. She had been given life when she had not asked for it, and simultaneously been denied any opportunity to transform that life into anything that she desired. She wanted the world, all of it. She wanted to drink it in, to make it part of her and her memories, but the torture of knowing that such freedom was impossible had driven her close to silent insanity. As she lived, her thoughts burned with the exasperation of all that was beyond her reach.

Their origins had doomed them forever, and they sat listlessly beside the ghost train, so still that anyone entering the haunted house would have taken them to be mere puppets without life or thoughts. Sir Lancelot tried again to think himself out of existence, except this time he was more cunning. He attempted to quiet his thoughts rather than force them into oblivion. He shut his eyes and listened to the silence, doing his upmost to let that silence become him, but all to no avail. His thoughts would not stop, and even if they paused for a moment they would come surging and dashing back, for there was terror in oblivion, and any time he happened to peer over that precipice every fibre of his being would rush to save him. Lady Godiva, curious about the actions of her companion and equally eager to purge herself of this thing called reality, closed her eyes and tried to be quiet too, but what followed surprised her. Instead of darkness all manner of images and an even greater array of thoughts bustled into her. She discovered that her mind was not only a living thing but an autonomous being, capable of thoughts which she had not summoned.

"Puppets!" the voice seemed to come from both nowhere and everywhere, echoing all around the haunted house from the mouths of the vampires, zombies and monsters slumped around the train tracks:

"I am the man who made you."

Once again Lady Godiva thought of God, and once again Mr Punch assured her that such ideas in such a world were fantasies. In the mad dash to escape the circus nobody had made any attempt to stop the ghost train, which continued to run circles around the room, materialising and vanishing down a smokey tunnel lit in fluorescent red hues. This also meant that all the associated pageantry of the ride, the skeleton that dropped from the ceiling when the train emerged from the tunnel, the bandage swaddled zombie which leapt from its coffin, and the several witches that cackled from the roof as the carriage passed by, were all in operation too. Surrounded by all these moving parts, it was difficult to discern from exactly where the voice had originated, but Mr Punch was convinced that it had its origins within the zombie.

"I will soon silence it" he said.

"Wait" Lady Godiva followed him, and Sir Lancelot followed Lady Godiva "He may be able to help."

"Puppets" the voice spoke again "You are wooden toys. I made you in my workshop."

Mr Punch let out a veritable shriek of rage, and for all Lady Godiva reached out to stop him, and for all Sir Lancelot reached out to protect her, he flew at the zombie and tore its bandages in a frenzy.

"Leave him" Sir Lancelot said in a hoarse whisper, for he dreaded that Mr Punch would fall upon Lady Godiva too.

The zombie did not put up any resistance whatsoever, but it took Mr Punch by surprise nonetheless. As he tore at the bandages he found that there were far more than he had expected. Layer upon layer of fabric ripped and tore from the body, but for some time there seemed to be nothing else underneath. He continued his frantic assault until the last of the bandages lay in a shredded pile on the floor and, instead of anything even vaguely human, all that remained was a wooden mannequin without even facial features. It was stiff and unmoving, but Mr Punch flung it to the ground and slammed the lid of its coffin closed regardless. The ghost train chugged by.

"I made you from wood" the disembodied voice continued "You are not real, living things and you never will be."

"I don't think it's coming from in here" said Sir Lancelot, for he was eager to stop the violence.

Mr Punch could not be placated though, because the voice was delivering the terrible truths which he dreaded the most, the truths which he had done his upmost to suppress since the first moments of consciousness. Sir Lancelot and Lady Godiva, stood side by side, felt those words reverberate inside them too. For Lady Godiva they were a stark reminder of all that she could never have, see or be, and for Sir Lancelot they were proof that he ought not to feel the tremendous love that he did, and that he was not designed to survive it. He was built to twitch on strings and nothing else. Mr Punch turned wildly on the spot, but the sound of the voice was echoing from several different directions at once.

"Damn it all" he said.

"Any feelings you have" continued the speaker "Are not real. They cannot be real. I carved you out of wood. Your thoughts are not real. Your feelings are not real."

The ghost train laboured slowly past again, a witch dropped from the roof to greet it, and Mr Punch, utterly in the grip of frenzy, leapt for the train and broke off the hand rail at the front. Brandishing it like a sword he took a wild swipe at the witch before its mechanism had chance to haul it back to the safety of the ceiling. He split the model cleanly in two, and a shower of straw fluttered miserably to the ground. That was not the source of the voice either. Only Lady Godiva understood, and she turned her back on the spectacle of Mr Punch, who was pacing to and fro with his iron bar, waiting for the next message or the next monster. She had realised that the voice could not possibly be coming from inside the haunted house, or indeed from inside the circus at all. It was coming from that great Outside which, with no prior knowledge and based only on hypothesis, she had concluded some time ago must be a real place filled with real people, real sights and the agonising promise of real life. The voice proved beyond any doubt that her predictions regarding the existence of an Outside beyond the red roof of the Big Top and the narrow corridors of the circus had been correct, and it only fuelled her desire to see it, to live in it and to be free. These desires burned within her as a torment, and she wondered where exactly in the Outside the voice was located, how it was projecting itself and who it belonged to. She wished to see and know, but she despaired at the words of the voice, for the truth it delivered was the truth of her captivity and the recurring sentence of her origins.

"First of all you were just blocks of wood" it continued "And then I carved out your bodies, attached your arms and your legs, and then painted your faces. I attached strings to your limbs because that is the only way that you can move. Someone has to operate you. You cannot move of your own accord. It is impossible. You are impossible. Abandon this fantasy."

Mr Punch let out a bellow of fury, and this time it was directed at a skeleton which hung on the edge of the tracks and would, on normal occasions, open its mouth and laugh manically as the train passed by. Mr Punch raised his iron bar and dealt it a terrific blow to the skull, which split and shattered at once. He then set about obliterating the remainder of the skeleton until it was nothing more than a pile of broken fragments. The train passed behind his back, its wheels sounding a moaning rhythm, and he turned, saw the model of some unidentifiable monster with red eyes and green scales and took a wild swing at that too. The bodies of the monsters in the haunted house were brittle indeed, and they collapsed without the least bit of resistance. Somewhere in his consciousness Mr Punch had long since reached the same conclusion as Lady Godiva, that the voice in no way had its source within the haunted house, but his rage at the words had blinded him, and he continued to hack this way and that, wielding his iron bar like a berserker.

Sir Lancelot and Lady Godiva looked down at themselves and knew perfectly well that the analysis of their anatomy was correct, and they recoiled in joint horror at the idea of alien hands attaching their arms and fastening their legs to their bodies. It was unbelievable, implausible and seemed to bear no connection to them, but the story of their genesis was plainly true. They vaguely recalled the strings, for they had torn them off in the first frantic moments of their lives. The sound of those strings tearing, as well as the sight of them, hanging limp from their bodies like creepers, had lingered in their minds as distant, rumbling thunder. All of this knowledge did not distance them from life though, rather it only served to emphasise the terror of the unreality from which they had inexplicably sprung. The dread that such a place still existed, and that they may one day return there, filled them with a terrific fear that made them feel more alive than ever.

"You are nothing more than puppets and you never will be. You can't be. Come out. Leave the circus and lie down in the field. I will come and collect you and take you back to my workshop, where you belong."

This was the final insult and Mr Punch, abandoning his assault upon the occupants of the haunted house, flung his iron bar high into the sky, where it crashed into the roof and stuck, imbedded in the ceiling.

"There is nothing" he said, and all the rage had drained from his voice.

The puppets did not materialise, and it was plain that the negotiation of the puppet maker had failed. Still, the police chief had finally found a little relief, because they had been able to reach the army. Reinforcements had been promised. Violence seemed to be the only recourse remaining. The silence emanating from the circus, coupled with the insult of the parrots, assured the police chief that any further attempts at negotiation would be utterly futile. He remained stood on the perimeter with the puppet maker by his side simply because there was nowhere else to go and nothing else to do, but he had begun to pin all his hopes upon the army. He imagined a huge platoon of rifles and cannons rolling into the circus and levelling the entire area, and he smiled at the thought of artillery, which would clatter into the tent and make short work of the puppets, reducing their wooden bodies to nothing but a bad memory. The explosive intervention of the army would be the talk of the town too, and everybody would soon forget about his own ineffectual vigil. When the army finally did arrive though, all they brought with them was yet another disappointment. No artillery came rumbling through the crowds, no horses, not even a platoon, just a lieutenant and three other soldiers with rifles slung across their backs. The police chief was a little relieved at the sight of khaki and helmets, but not much, and he let out an audible sigh of misery at the bedraggled troop, because all of a sudden it seemed as though even the army might not be enough. If the crisis were to slide into a second day his name and reputation would be in ruins. When the lieutenant came striding up to him he could not contain his frustration:

"I thought there would be more of you than this."

"These are all the soldiers we can spare."

The lieutenant was less than impressed at being called away at such a pivotal time, for there were rumours of a new and strange weapon, the likes of which had never been seen before and that could be deployed at any moment. It had been perfected over the course of the last week, or so the stories went. It seemed odd that puppets could be brought to life against such a back drop of strife, and especially that there had been no warning from military intelligence, whose only concern had been the weapon. He considered the role of local police officer so demeaning that it was almost an insult, and even if there had been any more soldiers to spare he would not have brought them. As it happened the three men behind him really were all that the army could muster, but everything about the situation; the ridiculously coloured Big Top, the hypnotic, rising and falling rhythm of the Ferris Wheel in the distance, the ring of overly curious, parasitic locals and the haggard face of the police chief, filled him with a rage that he had never experienced anywhere, not even on the battlefield. Provincialism of any kind disgusted him, and the idea that he would spend the afternoon engaged in a battle with children's puppets made him wonder whether the sleight was a deliberate one, and that he had offended high command in some way.

"Are you in charge here?" he barked at the police chief.

"Yes I am. I have-"

"And who is this?"

"I am the one who made the puppets" said the puppet maker "But I can assure you that none of this is anything-"

"You can go" the lieutenant waved him away, and the puppet maker, surprised that his ordeal had been concluded just like that, looked to the police chief for reassurance, but he only shrugged, and that seemed to be an end to the matter. The puppet maker was dismissed and returned home, hoping and praying to any force that would listen, that the half-constructed puppet he had left in his workshop would not have moved, and would still be there, reclining on his desk awaiting a face.

"And you" continued the lieutenant, his hand resting on the revolver in his belt "Can remove this crowd. I do not require an audience."

"I have tried that. We have made several efforts but they will not move."

"Then make them move. You have enough men here. Get rid of them at once. From now on I am in charge of this operation."

These were precisely the words that the chief of police had been longing to hear since the first mention of the animated puppets, for he had been desperately eager to shed this strange responsibility which he had been afflicted with, but now that it was finally gone he found himself quite stung. The lieutenant did not even linger long enough to see him go, and as he walked away the police chief called to one of the nearby officers, the youngest he had seen all day:

"Find me a stool to sit on!" and the boy dashed away to fulfil the command.

Meanwhile the lieutenant, without the slightest trace of fear, stepped over the police cordon and into the grounds of the circus. He did not even draw his gun, although he secretly hoped that somebody would fire a shot at him, if only so that he could fire back and vent some of his frustrations in battle. This was unlikely though, for he was knowledgeable in the ways of combat and he suspected that if the puppets had not shown their faces even once all afternoon, and only a single shot had been fired several hours ago, they were in fact trying to hide themselves and attempting to formulate a plan of escape. He continued to walk until he arrived at the coconut stand. The body of the slain clown took him somewhat by surprise, as he had not noticed it on his approach and it was rather more gory than he had expected. He crouched down in front of the body, peered into the bulging eyes, noted the long trail of blood which had streamed from the mouth and congealed on the fabric of the bright yellow blazer. The lieutenant felt nothing, not pity, not fear - not even surprise at how he could be so numb. Instead, the sight of the clown only reinforced to him the sheer ridiculousness of the situation he had been embroiled in, and he turned to the three soldiers who had been following, rifles in hand, a little distance behind. Before he spoke he noticed that the circus was actually far further from the town and the cordon of police than it had seemed. Instead of walking the short distance that he thought he had, it appeared as though he had travelled quite some way, and the crowd was tiny indeed. Still, even from this distance he could see that the local police had failed in the only task he had given them, for the locals were still there, watching his every move through eyes hungry for catastrophe. The puppets would have to be dealt with swiftly, and that would be an end to it. They were made of wood, and wood had one common enemy.

"Burn them" he gave the order to the soldiers "Burn them out. If there are any hostages then it is a shame, but that is how it goes in war."

The order was met with a chorus of "yes sirs," and the three soldiers were dispatched to find some tinder. The lieutenant did not go with them, rather he paced to and fro beside the body of the clown, wondering whether he ought to venture into the Big Top and overcome the puppets alone. This was not a desire for glory, for he had long since convinced himself that there was no glory to be found here, but rather a desire for action, for anything that would elevate this miserable duty above the mundane. Eventually the decision was made for him, because the three soldiers returned much quicker than he had expected and they began to build a fire, because in the end it does not matter what life is, who gave it to who or for what reason.

The puppets had abandoned the haunted house, for it had been the scene of some of their darkest revelations. The truths delivered by the puppet maker had seemed to be trapped amongst the mirrors, the monsters and the ghouls, so that the entire place became a home for living, tormenting thoughts which none of them had ever desired or asked for. With nothing else to do they allowed themselves to be led on, drawn by hidden impulses and obscure thoughts, back to the first place that they remembered, which was the circus ring beneath the imposing dome of the Big Top. It was here that Sir Lancelot heard the first whispers of the fire. They were sat miserably on the stage, just behind the curtain so that the rows of vacant seats were not visible, when a strange crackle, not unlike a menacing laugh, broke the silence.

"What was that?" and Lady Godiva got to her feet, ready to investigate.

"I will look" said Sir Lancelot, and he made his way out, passed the curtain and on to the stage.

At first it seemed as though nothing had changed. The circus ring, strewn with sand and the footprints of the deceased ringmaster, the gymnasts and the magicians, had not altered, and not a single soul remained in any of the seats. A new light, that of a dwindling day, had given everything a slightly darker, dusky hue, but for a few moments Sir Lancelot could not discern the source of the noise, and in those few moments it seemed as though everything in the world could simply continue, unchanging and indefinitely, until the final moment of time. It was then that he saw the first trace of a phantom. It slipped easily through the canvas entrance of the Big Top and then slid sinuously upwards, weaving and spinning in the air like a black snake. Sir Lancelot's fingers closed around the curtain and he gripped it tighter, for there was something in that sight, the vision of the ghost, which petrified him to the spot. The phantom slithered upwards, and it was lengthy indeed, for it continued to flow through the entrance in an unbroken stream, always more, and always upwards, spiralling towards the roof where it was unable to travel any further and instead remained trapped, swirling and eddying this way and that. The smoke drifted softly across the ceiling and, ushered on by the hidden undulations of the breeze, twisted and contorted into strange and unusual shapes which seemed almost human, as though they had a life of their own and were holding council in the ceiling of the Big Top. Sir Lancelot watched them with vague, uneasy concern, for he had never encountered smoke or fire, and he certainly had no idea that his brittle frame would succumb so easily to flame, but some innate sense told him to be afraid. The smoke continued to congregate and dance, except now it had crept directly above his head and was beginning to descend as though it truly was alive, as though it was thinking, scheming, and coming to destroy him of its own accord.

"Mr Punch…?" he said cautiously, eager that somebody else should witness this mass movement which filled him with such an odd, unspeakable fear.

Mr Punch did not materialise though, and Sir Lancelot was left alone as the smoke continued to mass. The whole of the Big Top was wrapped in a dark haze, and it was increasingly difficult to see from one end to the other. Most of the smoke had risen to the ceiling, but now it was crowding into the ring, around the seats, and the circus was not empty, but filled with hundreds of swirling, whispering ghosts which cackled and sighed with malicious intent. All at once there was fire, too, just a single spark which crackled at the entrance to the Big Top, leapt inside and then pounced on the fabric walls, and suddenly Sir Lancelot, for no reason whatsoever, knew all that there was to know about fire; what it was and how it spread like a starving wolf, guzzling everything in its path. He knew, too, what it would do to him if it could catch him in its jaws.

"Fire" and Mr Punch was at his side "There will be no escaping that."

Mr Punch did not linger long to watch the spreading of the fire, which was occurring at pace. That first spark had leapt and caught the canvas of the Big Top and then begun to spread, creeping upwards to join the smoke in the roof. Sir Lancelot watched his great nemesis as it conquered the circus on its inexorable path towards him, creeping and laughing its way through the ring, and all the while whispering and taunting as though it knew all the secrets of his being. He discovered that he could not watch the flames because they recalled him to the strange oblivion which had existed before his birth into life, that incomprehensible nothingness which inspired in him vertigo, and made him reach for the curtain to steady himself.

Behind the curtain Mr Punch was speaking.

"We have missed our opportunity to hurt them, although we did a little damage before our memories properly began" he said "Now it is too late and we are doomed without even the prospect of revenge. It is for the best."

Sir Lancelot was inclined to agree with him, for the pain that he felt for Lady Godiva was growing close to unbearable, and even Lady Godiva sensed that Mr Punch was correct, for there was nothing she could do, nowhere she could go, only wish and be tormented by a world that was far beyond her. Mr Punch could not be still, and he paced this way and that as he spoke:

"We have nowhere to go. We may as well wait and burn with the circus. It's where we came from."

Nobody spoke, and Mr Punch emitted a low, hollow laugh that echoed in his empty chest. He looked Sir Lancelot directly in the eye:

"Do you have anything to continue for?"

"Not a thing" he replied truthfully. Even if he were to spend an eternity beside Lady Godiva it would make no difference, because he had no words for her, nothing at all, and he knew that the towering feelings within would destroy him whatever the case.

"And you?" Mr Punch turned his scorching gaze upon Lady Godiva.

"Nothing" she said "There is so much, but nothing for me."

"Nothing for any of us" said Mr Punch, and then after a pause "That's an end to it then."

When they left their enclave behind the curtain to sit on the stage, the flames had already consumed much of the Big Top. Mr Punch regretted that he had been unable to hurt his creator and wreak revenge upon the puppet maker for giving him this body and placing him in this terrible situation of life. Even that did not matter though, because the flames would empty him of his regrets, and he wondered whether, in the final moments before he disintegrated, he would know what it is to be at peace. Sir Lancelot wondered the same thing, for he knew that the fire would liberate him from this peculiar world of peculiar and tremendous feelings. Even Lady Godiva looked to the flames with gratitude as they swamped the circus, for they would be an end to all her impossible dreams. Time was fleeting and impossible, for the fire would not delay itself for anybody. Mr Punch ran headlong into the flames, for there was no fear in him, only the hope of solace that his wooden body and wooden mind would be punished and purged for all that they were. Sir Lancelot sat a little longer, dreaming of Lady Godiva but comforted by the knowledge that it was all over, that his feelings would perish with him and that he was perfectly free to dream of her, for it was all without consequence: he was free to love without the fear of pain. He imagined himself walking by her side beneath the moon and the stars and smiled, not because it would happen, but because it did not matter.

Lady Godiva had fallen back a little to hide herself from the demise of her companions, but the curtain finally caught fire and collapsed in a flurry of sparks and flame, revealing the whole sorry scene. Everything was ablaze: the seats, the ring, the roof, the canvas walls, everything - and both Mr Punch and Sir Lancelot were gone. Thick black smoke billowed and swirled like a sooty, toxic sea, bulging and eddying through the Big Top. Lady Godiva was entirely alone in the world, and as the flames climbed higher she thought of her dreams and her hope of freedom. She did her upmost to convince herself that it was all impossible, that all she could do was feed herself to the oblivion of the flames, but she could not quite abandon her fantasies. As the first soldier, his rifle cocked and ready to fire, came rushing into view through the collapsing canopy she knew very well that this was the time to surrender to the inferno. It would only have taken a few steps, a small effort so tiny in comparison to the frenetic, terrified struggle against oblivion which she recalled in the first moments of her existence, and she would be ashes like Mr Punch and Sir Lancelot. She told herself again and again that she ought to be ashes, that she must be ashes, and that it was all she could be. She did her upmost to convince herself that the wide world which had somehow crowded, fully formed into her mind, was entirely inaccessible to her, with her wooden origins and wooden heart, but she could not quite do it. Suddenly and inexplicably the great loneliness she felt at the demise of Mr Punch and Sir Lancelot was not a loneliness at all, but a type of freedom, for she had been liberated from the tyranny of Mr Punch's rage and even the hopeless melancholy of Sir Lancelot. This revelation was followed by a second, and she knew that if the circus were set to burn to the ground, then the canvas walls, the narrow corridors and the locked doors would cease to be as well. It may all be impossible: the dream of freedom and the dream of hope. All the rich hues of existence may well be far beyond her reach, but they would be even further away should she give herself to the fire. The decision, the first which was truly her own, stunned her so much that for a few moments she forgot her wooden body, her wooden mind and her wooden origins. She forgot even the fire, and she did not move. A flaming rafter clattered from the roof, but as soon as she had made the decision to be free she found that the whole world was suddenly on her side, and the object of doom missed Lady Godiva by several feet. Another one of the soldiers came charging through the smoke and raised his gun, but he was aiming at the lion, which had escaped its cage in the carnage, and when he fired he missed even that, as it bounded away through the fire. Lady Godiva was free, utterly free, and as the circus burned she slipped away.

They could not put the fire out, and that night the sky was dyed a sickly shade of crimson, so that it seemed as though a great plague hung over the world, ready to descend at any moment.

The End.

MORE BOOKS FROM DAVID JONES

Love & Space Dust. A Poetry Anthology.

Love & Space Dust is a poetry anthology exploring love and eternity. Timeless poetry of feeling and emotion, Love & Space Dust carries readers on a journey through love, life and relationships, and then far beyond, into the stars and the far flung galaxies, where all that remains of the feelings we once felt and the lives we once lived is love and space dust.

"After spending over ten years in a literature club and hearing/reading more poems than I could count, I thought I had seen it all. I have never been so wrong. Love and Space Dust contains so many beautifully written poems that brought tears to my eyes that I didn't put my Kindle down until I had read every single one of them at least twice." Amazon.de Customer Review.

"Lovely book." Amazon.com Customer Review

"I really enjoy all of the poems. They make you feel like never before. By far some of my favorite poems." Amazon.com Customer Review.

"LOVED LOVED LOVED THIS!!" Goodreads Review.

"These poems are so full of Pain and Darkness, but so full of Hope and Light." Amazon.de Customer Review.

"This book is absolutely amazing and i hope there will be more to come!" Amazon.com Customer Review

"Love this book so much!" Goodreads Review.

"Made me smile and moved me to tears." Amazon.co.uk Customer Review.

Could You Ever Live Without? A Poetry Anthology.

Poems of feeling and experience, the anthology encompasses all of life and beyond: death, the universe, hopes, dreams, love, loss - all of existence contained in one work. Poetry that captures both moments and lifetimes, memories and hopes, reality and dreams. Poems to identify with, poems of life.

"Take it from a non-poetry reader: this book is a gem, destined to become timeless." Amazon Customer Review.

"Loved the poems, a very great read. Once I started reading it was hard to stop." Amazon Customer Review.

"This book is beautiful. It's one of my most cherished possessions." Amazon Customer Review.

"Not all poetry is worth reading. This is." Amazon Customer Review.

"A great reflection of the deeper thoughts from this generation." Amazon Customer Review.

"Beautiful collection of poetry, I'm not an avid poetry reader but this book is absolutely stunning." Amazon.co.uk Customer Review.

"Everytime I read this book I find new meanings." Goodreads Review.

Love As The Stars Went Out. A Poetry Anthology.

A collection of poetry from the end of the world. Poems of love, feeling and emotion, the collection encompasses all of life, and even beyond. Simple and elegant, the book contains all the poetry of existence.

"This book is amazing I would really recommend getting the other two as well they are some of my favourite books of all time." Amazon.co.uk Customer Review.

"I love every bit of this book. So simple yet deep meaningful words. I would recommend it to all and everyone...." Amazon.com Customer Review.

"Five stars. Awesome book." Amazon.com Customer Review.

"Such a beautiful piece." Amazon.com Customer Review.

Death's Door. A novella of love, life and death.

"She was like the dawn, insubstantial and somehow transient, as though she would fade from reality at any moment."

Every day the villagers watch as Death, a spectral suit of black armour mounted upon a horse, rides through the valley beneath their mountain top home. After a lifetime living on the edge of Death's domain, his close proximity is neither terrible or threatening, rather he has become a simple fact of life and a familiar neighbour. Nothing seems to change until one night a young boy, alone in the meadows beneath a summer moon, watches a mysterious figure in white approaching the village through the tall grass.

"A spectacular novella, a quick read but engaging and thoughtful. The story carries you as swift as death's horse does." Amazon.com Customer Review.

"Buy this book! Great teen-based book. Even better for post teen (aka 55 year old father) reader." Amazon.com Customer Review.

"This book quickly became my forever favorite. You will not regret buying it. Although it's about death himself, it has so much to teach about life." Amazon.com Customer Review.

Highway Heart. My newest poetry collection.

Highway Heart is a collection of over one hundred poems on relationships, life and the universe. The theme is journeys - the travel we undertake in life, the type of internal travel which traces roads inside our hearts.

Half an exploration of the difficulties of finding the right path in life, and half a bitter sweet celebration of the myriad of strange, exciting, heartbreaking and unexpected roads we discover for ourselves, Highway Heart is above all else the poetic tale of a journey.

"This is one of the greatest works I've ever read. This is truly, truly, a masterpiece. I hope it gets more recognition in the future. Please, please read it, it will touch the deepest parts of your heart." Amazon.com Review.

And Coming Soon...

A full length novel by David Jones exploring themes of love, eternity, the nature of the universe and history.

"When all of this is over, will our atoms play amongst the stars? Will we dance and laugh through the galaxies? Will we be happy at last?"

For further information and news on the novel please visit:

Twitter: @djthedavid
Instagram: @storydj
Youtube: youtube.com/storydj
Facebook: facebook.com/davidjoneswriter

Made in the USA
Monee, IL
16 July 2023

39283398R10142